Cutting Taxes for Insuring

AEI STUDIES ON TAX REFORM

Kevin A. Hassett

Series Editor

ASSESSING THE EFFECTIVENESS OF SAVING INCENTIVES

R. Glenn Hubbard and Jonathan S. Skinner

CUTTING TAXES FOR INSURING: OPTIONS AND EFFECTS
OF TAX CREDITS FOR HEALTH INSURANCE

Mark V. Pauly and Bradley Herring

DISTRIBUTIONAL IMPLICATIONS OF A CONSUMPTION TAX

William M. Gentry and R. Glenn Hubbard

THE EFFECTS OF RECENT TAX REFORM ON LABOR SUPPLY

Thomas J. Kniesner and James P. Ziliak

FUNDAMENTAL ISSUES IN CONSUMPTION TAXATION

David F. Bradford

FUNDAMENTAL TAX REFORM AND CORPORATE FINANCE

William M. Gentry and R. Glenn Hubbard

TAX POLICY AND INVESTMENT

Kevin A. Hassett

TAXATION OF FINANCIAL SERVICES
UNDER A CONSUMPTION TAX

Peter R. Merrill

TAXING CONSUMPTION IN A GLOBAL ECONOMY

Harry Grubert and T. Scott Newlon

TAXING INTERNATIONAL BUSINESS INCOME:
DIVIDEND EXEMPTION VERSUS THE CURRENT SYSTEM

Harry Grubert and John Mutti

Cutting Taxes for Insuring

Options and Effects of Tax Credits for Health Insurance

Mark V. Pauly
and
Bradley Herring

The AEI Press

Publisher for the American Enterprise Institute

WASHINGTON, D.C.

2002

To order call toll free 1-800-462-6420 or 1-717-794-3800.
For all other inquiries please contact the AEI Press, 1150 Seventeenth Street, N.W.,
Washington, D.C. 20036 or call 1-800-862-5801.

ISBN 978-0-8447-7160-1

1 3 5 7 9 10 8 6 4 2

The AEI Press
Publisher for the American Enterprise Institute
1150 17th Street, N.W.
Washington, D.C. 20036

Contents

Foreword

Economists have reached a broad consensus concerning the appearance of an optimal tax system. Such a system would have a very broad base—perhaps limited to consumption—and marginal tax rates as low as revenue demands will allow. While there is general agreement concerning those basic features of an optimal tax system, significant disagreement remains concerning the size of the benefits to be gained from a fundamental reform that would replace the current system of high marginal tax rates with one that conformed closely to the prescriptions of theory. Disagreement also abounds concerning the distributional impact of fundamental tax reforms. The lack of professional consensus undoubtedly discourages would-be reformers, who for more than a decade have shied away from fundamental fixes and instead tinkered endlessly with a system that has increased steadily in complexity.

With this state of affairs in mind, we at AEI have organized a tax reform seminar series since January 1996. At each seminar, an economist presents original research designed to bring consensus concerning the costs and benefits of fundamental tax reform one step closer. Recent topics include transition problems in moving to a consumption tax, the effects of consumption taxation on housing and the stock market, the distributional impact of tax reforms, the effect of privatizing Social Security on the long-term budget outlook, and the international tax implications of fundamental reform.

The goal of this pamphlet series is to distribute the best research on economic issues in tax reform to as broad an audience as possible. Each publication reflects not only the insights of the authors, but also the helpful comments and criticisms of seminar participants—economists, attorneys, accountants, and journalists in the tax policy community.

KEVIN A. HASSETT
American Enterprise Institute

Acknowledgments

This research was supported by a grant from the Leon Lowenstein Foundation. A previous version of this paper, "Using Tax Policy to Reduce the Number of Uninsured," was prepared for a conference held on December 17, 1999, by the Council on the Economic Impact of Health System Change.

1

Introduction

Despite rising real incomes, the number of uninsured workers and dependents has not fallen appreciably. Workers sometimes choose jobs at which no employment-based coverage is offered, and then fail to purchase individual coverage as a substitute, or they reject group insurance when it is offered to them at a fraction of its total premium. In response, policymakers in both political parties have considered the use of tax credits to encourage the purchase of private insurance coverage.

A tax credit for health insurance would reduce the federal income and payroll taxes of a worker who obtains health insurance. Most proposals envision a refundable tax credit that would pay cash to a person who purchases insurance but has a federal tax liability less than the value of the credit.

In this essay we focus on the distributional and allocative effects of a variety of forms of tax credits. We describe the relative effects in qualitative terms and provide some estimates of their quantitative magnitude. We limit our analysis primarily to workers and their dependents, who constitute the great bulk of the uninsured and who are falling beyond the reach of the current tax subsidy given to employment-based health insurance. We also investigate workers whose incomes place them above the poverty line but below the median family income; this group, with incomes too high for traditional subsidy programs but too low to provide generous funding for insurance, are most difficult to reach with traditional welfare programs and yet make up the great bulk of the uninsured.

Most tax credit proposals direct new subsidies to different people from those whose insurance purchases have been subsidized in the past, and the credits differ in amount, design, and required spending from those credits with which the nation already has some experience. We know how moderate tax subsidies (for employer-paid premiums) affect insurance purchases by the middle class and above, and we know how massive subsidies (through Medicaid) affect the coverage of the poor. But most tax credit proposals envision subsidies larger than moderate but less than massive, and would target those subsidies on the great bulk of the uninsured who have incomes between poor and the median income. Policymakers should therefore be humble in estimating the effect of any single plan and, in choosing among plans, prefer designs that accommodate a wide range of possible but currently unknowable outcomes over designs whose effects are very efficient or equitable in some circumstances but very skewed under others.

Our conclusions differ from those of more conventional analyses in two ways. First, we find plausible effects on the numbers of uninsured persons that are larger than those of other studies. Second, we focus explicitly on the distinction between the "cost" to the federal government of tax credits (based on the usual accounting for tax credit programs) and the more relevant measures of tax credits' effects on aggregate economic welfare and cost to the economy in terms of the reallocation of resources. Using this perspective, some tax credit programs with "net costs to the federal government" greater than the premium per newly insured person actually have true economic costs that are quite low. We believe economic cost, not cost to the government, is the most appropriate measure to use when comparing different tax credit policies. Nevertheless, we still find (as do most other studies) that modest subsidies will have little effect in reducing the number of the uninsured; subsidies may have to be on the order of 50 percent of premiums to have any important effect. Beyond that threshold, however, the effect can be substantial.

The Features of a Tax Credit Program

The key features of a tax credit program are

- the dollar amounts of credits for which a person with a given set of characteristics is eligible

- the amount or type of insurance to which the credit may be applied

- eligibility requirements for people with different characteristics

For example, one simple type of credit program would make a fixed dollar amount of credit available for a specified benchmark insurance policy to all workers and their dependents at a given income level. If the premium for the benchmark policy were $2,500 per worker per year and the credit was, say, $1,000 for every uninsured worker, we would want to know what fraction of those persons would prefer to pay $1,500 for the benchmark policy rather than remaining uninsured. That is, how many people have "reservation prices" for insurance above and below $1,500? One simple type of estimate would assume that a worker whose expected out-of-pocket "insurable" medical expenses exceeded $1,500 would surely have a reservation price of $1,500 or more and therefore would prefer the credit to remaining uninsured. In addition, there may might be other risk-averse persons with lower expected losses who would seek insurance with the subsidy. Still other design features and motivations to value insurance should be considered. A primary reason credits have small effects, we find, is that the out-of-pocket expenses of the uninsured, even the uninsured with incomes well above the poverty line, are not very large on average.

A Benchmark Case and Some Descriptive Statistics

The characteristics of the uninsured vary substantially. Substantial fractions of the uninsured are both high and low income, both young and middle-aged, both in good health and in frail or poor health. To make clear the tradeoffs in different tax credit designs, we begin by focusing on a subset of the uninsured population that is both relevant to policy and more homogenous than the uninsured population as a whole, namely, full-time workers and their dependents.

We have selected this population for several reasons. Workers and their dependents make up a majority of the uninsured, yet are eligible for larger subsidies under the present tax code than any other group that is neither poor nor elderly. Since the working uninsured have passed up significant subsidies already, even larger subsidies will likely be needed to get the attention of this population and motivate them to obtain coverage.

In addition, we begin by examining the subset of workers and dependents whose total family incomes lie between 200 and 250 percent of the federal poverty line, adjusted for family size. This population with incomes just above twice the poverty line represents the lower middle class, who have the most difficult time obtaining insurance. Their incomes are too high for substantial Medicaid subsidies (although they have been targeted for the Children's Health Initiative Program in some states). They cannot expect to obtain a significant amount of charity care except in the case of severe illnesses; most of the time they should expect to pay something. And yet they have little discretionary income to spend on medical care or on individual, "nongroup" insurance.

Table 1 provides some descriptive statistics both for the entire U.S. population of workers and their dependents and for this lower-middle-income sub-sample, based on the large nationwide 1996 Medical Expenditure Panel Survey (MEPS). While a majority of those between 200 and 250 percent of poverty do obtain private insurance in some fashion, about 22 percent of such individuals without public coverage are entirely uninsured—somewhat in excess of the national average proportion for workers. As expected, the proportion covered by public insurance is small, less than 10 percent of the total, some portion of which represents retired military. Of the uninsured workers and dependents at this income level, about 42 percent have a family member who was offered insurance in connection with his employment, declined it, and failed to obtain nongroup insurance—also in excess of the national average of about 38 percent. The remaining 58 percent of these lower-middle-income uninsured have no family member who took a job at which insurance was offered.[1] Of the insured, 94 percent obtain their coverage through an employer, while only 6 percent have purchased private nongroup coverage.

Why did a sizable minority fail to obtain coverage? We can rule out some explanations. One common hypothesis is that they could not "afford" coverage—presumably meaning that the purchase of insurance would leave too little income for other necessities. We know of no technical economic definition of "affordable," but income alone cannot explain the failure to purchase insurance, because a majority of persons at the same income level did somehow obtain coverage. Another possibility is that workers not offered job-based coverage found the high loading or stricter underwriting of individual insurers to be a barrier. Since the data we are using were taken from a time in which the unemployment rate was low, many of these workers would have had the opportunity to choose another job that did carry group coverage, but for some reason chose instead a job with no coverage but higher money wages. Moreover, recent research suggests the individual insurance market is neither as prone to rejecting high risks nor as costly as many suppose (Pauly and Herring 1999, Pauly et al. 1999). On the other hand, the same research finds that lower-income employees of small firms who were high risks were more likely to lack coverage than others of similar income, and that the combination of relatively high administrative loading and no tax subsidy makes individual insurance unattractive (even if it is not "unaffordable").

These results suggest that low income and high insurance prices don't entirely explain the failure by members of this population group to obtain insurance for themselves and their dependents. The desire for insurance may be weak, public or charity care opportunities may exist, expected expenses may be low, or unusually pressing family financial needs may make the premium the uninsured would be willing to pay—their reservation price—substantially less than the lowest premium they can find.

While determining these "other reasons" would be highly useful research, we assume here that the distribution of reservation prices is given. We then estimate what proportion of persons would have reservation prices below the price of insurance after it was reduced by a given tax credit program.

Before considering the effects of new subsidy programs, however, we need to describe the pattern of subsidies currently received by this group. The largest proportion of such subsidies involves the exclusion of employer-paid premiums for group insurance from income and payroll taxes (at federal and state levels). Persons who are not wage earners have virtually zero federal income tax deductibility for insurance premiums, because they rarely have enough medical expenses and other deductibles to make it worthwhile to itemize such deductions when paying their income tax. Self-employed persons may deduct a portion of their premiums, but again the low proportion of itemizing taxpayers in this income category makes such behavior rare. Still, people in this group have some opportunities to receive free or subsidized care, through public hospitals, the Veterans Administration, neighborhood health centers, and the like.

Consider the following example: a single, middle-aged, male wage earner with total compensation of $20,000 a year, which gives him a marginal federal income tax rate of 15 percent and places him between 200 and 250 percent of the poverty line. If he is uninsured, or even purchases nongroup insurance, his net federal tax is $4,604 (income tax of $3,004, plus an 8 percent payroll tax of $1,600). By contrast, let us consider a similar worker whose employer offers insurance and covers 80 percent of a typical single-coverage premium of $1,847[2] with full incidence on wages: He pays taxes of $4,268 (income tax of $2,779, plus payroll tax of $1,489). The tax exemption for employer-paid insurance, in other words, provides our second hypothetical worker a subsidy of $336, which is 1.7 percent of his income and 7.3 percent of his tax liability. The magnitude of this subsidy—equal to the employer-paid portion of a worker's insurance premium multiplied by his marginal tax rate—increases as one's income rises.[3]

This regressive subsidy has implications for efficiency in designing tax credits and for estimating the effectiveness of alternative subsidy programs. The ideally efficient subsidy program would offer the same subsidy to a person with given characteristics in different settings. Unfortunately, the present subsidy induces people to choose group insurance more frequently than its costs and benefits to them justify, to choose excessive amounts of insurance coverage, and to choose different employment arrangements from their most efficient ones.

The present tax subsidy also affects any new subsidy program. Many (though not all) of the currently uninsured could have taken advantage of the current subsidy. The most important way they could have done so (but chose not to) would have been to take a job at a firm offering insurance with full or partial employer payment of premiums. They might also have refused insurance because of a positive employee premium at a firm that made insurance available. If, then, the uninsured population contains disproportionate numbers of persons who have rejected coverage at the current subsidy, it follows that they will only purchase coverage (if at all) if they receive a subsidy larger than the current subsidy. And so any new subsidy program must offer a subsidy to each income group larger than the subsidy, or net insurance cost, currently available to them through the tax advantages of employment-based insurance. In short, effective new subsidies must be relatively large because they must "climb over" the existing, relatively generous subsidies.

Design Options

Consider individuals whose expected medical expenses are similar. Because of other influences, such as different aversions to risk, their willingness to pay (or reservation price) for a given insurance policy will vary. Given a particular insurance premium charged in the market for a standard policy, persons with reservation prices greater than the market price will purchase the policy, but those with reservation prices less than the market premium will not and so will be uninsured. If the government then provides a fixed-dollar tax credit for the purchase of the benchmark policy, some formerly uninsured persons will also purchase it. The reduction in the number of uninsured persons will depend on the number of people whose reservation prices are between the original market price and that price minus the credit.

If the purchase of at least a minimum benchmark policy is required in order to qualify for the fixed-dollar credit, some persons with high marginal values for insurance may choose to purchase additional coverage beyond that level (depending on the market price for additional coverage). But such choices will fully reflect the additional cost (assuming the insurance market is competitive) and therefore will be efficient.

Those persons who had already been purchasing insurance before the credit was offered may also be expected to claim the credit, and the total tax credits given by the government will exceed the amount of credits claimed by the formerly uninsured. This "excess credit" is not an inefficient allocation of resources. If the credit is viewed as public spending, its cost to the government per newly insured person is high. But if the credit paid to those already purchasing insurance is viewed as a tax reduction for them, then the situation simply involves giving equal tax treatment to all those in the eligible group who purchase insurance. Assuming that the purchase of insurance is responsible behavior, we may describe the plan as one that gives equal tax cuts to everyone who engages in responsible behavior. Either way, the credit paid to those who had already been purchasing insurance does not reallocate productive resources from the private to the public sector.

Compared to uninsured persons with equal levels of total compensation, persons who purchase insurance have less to spend on other goods, since they have chosen to divert more of their compensation to health insurance. They and their families may even suffer other deprivations (less decent housing, less educational spending) than those who take jobs with employers who do not reduce wages in order to pay for insurance. If we knew the impact of obtaining insurance on other aspects of families' spending, we might well judge the insured lower-income person to be more deserving of a tax reduction than a similar worker who is uninsured.

Now suppose that expected expenses and premiums under the benchmark policy vary across potential insurance purchasers; that is, there is variation in "risk." A uniform dollar credit should affect insurance purchasing in inverse proportion to the individual risk-level, so that persons at low risk of incurring medical expenses are the most likely to buy insurance with the help of the credit. For the sake of equity, however, we may want to vary the credit with the degree of risk involved; it may also be desirable to do so for those whose risk is so high that income effects (in terms of the value of the premium relative to total income) are large enough to seriously affect their likelihood of insurance purchasing.

Now suppose the benchmark policy is altered so that it is less comprehensive and therefore carries a lower premium. If the credit were kept at the same level, higher proportions of the relevant population would buy some insurance. The average level of coverage per insured person would fall, but the proportion of people without any insurance at all would also fall. Whether the average level of coverage per person eligible would rise or fall is unclear. In the limit, if the minimum policy's premium equaled the credit (or, equivalently, if the only requirement to qualify for the credit was buying a policy that cost at least as much as the credit), one would expect everyone to become insured. Insurance is free. No out-of-pocket premium would be required, and insurance of any positive amount should be worth something.

An alternative to a fixed-dollar or "closed end" tax credit is a credit that is a specified proportion of the policy premium (for instance, 25 percent). If a single benchmark policy is eligible for credit and the individual risk-level is uniform, there is no difference between a proportional credit and a fixed-dollar credit equal to this proportion times the benchmark policy's premium. In the more reasonable case in which the benchmark policy is only a minimum, and matching payments continue to be made for the premiums of more generous coverage, proportional credits are inefficient because they encourage additional coverage worth less than its cost. But proportional credits are a partial (though very crude) substitute for risk adjustment. They are also appropriate if some positive social value is attached to additional coverage beyond the minimum benchmark level.

Who in the population of lower-middle-income workers and dependents might be made eligible for tax credits? We assume that it will never be desirable to offer credits only to those currently uninsured. While this might work the first time, eventually it will provide everyone with incentives to drop coverage so as to be eligible for the credit.

There are two practical options here. One is to make eligible for credits at a given income level only those who currently are not offered employment-based insurance. The other is to make every worker at that income level eligible. In this latter case, someone who receives a credit could not at the same time receive the benefit of the tax exclusion of any employer payments; such payments must somehow be added to taxable income before computing the credit.

The second option makes credits attractive to all workers for whom receiving the credit is more advantageous than paying taxes on the amount no longer excluded. The first option offers an incentive for workers for whom the credit is more attractive than the exclusion to move to jobs in which no employer-paid insurance is offered. If some workers currently offered employment-based insurance for whom the credit is more attractive choose not to change their situations, the total amount of tax credits paid will be less than in the situation in which the credit is offered to all workers who choose it.

It is plausible that, at least in the short run, workers currently offered insurance who would gain from the credit may fail to change their situation. Changing jobs or replacing the employer payments with wage income will be inconvenient for some, and inefficient for others. The main tradeoff between these two options is therefore a lower level of tax credit payments when eligibility is limited, traded off against sometimes-strong incentives to change jobs or restructure the mix of compensation between money wages and paid health benefits. In some cases, an existing group insurance plan might be a casualty of the tax-credit-induced switch away from an employer-paid tax exclusion option. The other consideration (not really a tradeoff) is that the higher credit payments to those already purchasing insurance (all formerly insured workers under the first option, those who were buying nongroup coverage under the second) are transfers that are unequivocally more equitable than limiting the credit to those who were formerly uninsured. Those who had been purchasing insurance would be making the same or greater sacrifice to obtain coverage as those formerly uninsured who receive the credit and then purchase; they therefore deserve to pay the same net taxes. The only sense in which it is "inefficient" to subsidize those who were formerly insured is if the social objective is the welfare of those who manage (or are responsible for) the federal budget.

Still, we should note that accepting a fixed credit that is less in dollar amount than the value of the exclusion one currently experiences may be desirable if the policy that can be obtained with the credit is more attractive than the policy associated with the exclusion. A policy could be more attractive either because it represents a different type of insurance (e.g., *not* a managed care plan) or because the employee's total net premium payment is lower than that for the policy associated with the exclusion. In a sense, the number of people who turn in expensive exclusions for cheaper credit would be a measure of the distortion presently caused by the exclusion.

2

Estimating the Effects of Tax Credits

There has been an explosion of efforts to estimate both how many net new persons would be induced to become insured under various tax credit proposals and also the resulting total value of tax reductions caused by the availability of credits. In what follows we offer some estimates based on traditional approaches and some estimates that are novel because they are the only ones we know of that are explicitly based on a theory and data that determine which persons will be better off by choosing credits rather than by remaining uninsured. We call our estimates "synthetic" because they are based on models of choice of those workers made eligible for credits under specific credit proposals, rather than estimated from behavior of possibly (but not necessarily) similar consumers in situations similar (but not really identical) to those that would prevail under a particular tax credit plan.

One key insight in our approach is based on the observation that the great bulk of the working uninsured had an opportunity to obtain group insurance coverage at tax-subsidized prices but rejected it. Since they chose not to take advantage of that opportunity, it is highly likely that their reservation price is below the price they could have paid but did not. It follows that any tax credit proposal will only become effective if it can reduce the net premium for insurance below the level that prevailed in the rejected opportunity.

Suppose, for example, that we consider a worker in an occupation in which the typical firm size is twenty workers, and suppose this worker's marginal tax rate (income plus payroll) is 23 percent. Suppose that the loading for this size group is 30 percent of premiums. The net loading this person might expect to pay is therefore approximately 7 percent of premiums. Suppose finally that we observe that the person remains uninsured—because he had chosen a job in a firm that does not offer benefits.

If we assume that this worker could have worked in a typical firm that did offer benefits and chose not to do so because he preferred the higher wages or other advantages of his current job, we could conclude that this person's reservation price is below the net premium. With a tax credit applicable to individual insurance with loading assumed to be 40 percent of premiums, this person will surely not use the credit if it does not reduce the net loading on that policy even further. If it does not offset this much of the nongroup premium, the only reason to use it is if the nongroup policy is more to the person's tastes than any group offering. In this particular example, using the credit will only become generally attractive when it covers about a third of the nongroup premium. That is to say, the credit has to be large enough to match the rejected tax subsidy-group loading combination before it can begin to make a serious dent in the numbers of uninsured. If one's marginal tax rate is higher or the group is larger than in the example, the credit will have to be larger still to become effective.

This story obviously permits of exceptions. On the one hand, there may be those with reservation prices above the tax subsidized group price but below the unsubsidized nongroup insurance price who are "trapped" in jobs where no insurance is offered, even though they would willingly accept lower wages to pay for it. While some percentage of uninsured workers would surely purchase coverage if they were offered it at the tax-subsidized group premium but are unable to obtain a job that offers insurance in exchange for lower wages, there may be some individuals, on the other hand, who would prefer to be uninsured but are "trapped" at jobs which offer insurance. Indeed, some uninsured workers (about 20 percent on average), are at firms at which group insurance is offered but with employee premiums (Cooper and Schone 1997); for them, the reservation price of insurance must be below the employee premium.

3

Two Models, Two Estimates

We will now illustrate likely responses to various amounts and types of tax credits to describe actual and potential insurance purchasing in response to tax and other subsidies and price changes. The first method we develop uses employment and insurance status data from individuals in the first round of the 1996 Medical Expenditure Panel Survey (MEPS) to impute the proportions of individuals purchasing insurance at various "net" prices. The second method we develop uses medical expenditure data from the same survey to attempt to determine reservation prices of the uninsured more directly.

Our first method is more closely related to the theory outlined above. We determine for each family with at least one full-time worker the average net loading they would face in the group market given their job (or the nongroup market for the self-employed) and determine the proportion insured at each level of net loading. Specifically, we first determine the median number of workers per firm for each of twelve industries identified in the MEPS, and then, using estimates for group insurance loading by firm size in Phelps (1997), determine each worker's average administrative loading based upon the industry in which they are employed. We define four different average firm sizes, with values for administrative loading between 15 and 30 percent of benefits. Then, for each family, we determine the administrative loading they face (the lower of the two for dual-earner couples) and their marginal tax rate (income plus payroll) based upon their total family income and family structure; here, there are six different marginal income tax rates ranging from 0 to 39.6 percent, with 8 percent payroll added to each.

We represent the net loading relative to benefits (commonly termed the "price" of insurance) each family currently faces as $L_N =$ $(1 - Et)(1 + L_A) - 1$ where L_A is this administrative loading as a proportion of expected benefits, E is the average fraction of the premium paid by the employer (based upon summary data from the MEPS Insurance Component), and t is the family's marginal tax rate. For families with only self-employed workers, the net loading they currently face is simply the administrative loading in the nongroup market, which we assume to be either 30 percent of premiums ($L_N \cong 0.429$) or 40 percent of premiums ($L_N \cong 0.667$).

We then consider the effect of a tax credit defined as a given proportion of the total nongroup premium; that is, a credit essentially risk-adjusted equivalently to whatever risk characteristics the individual insurance market uses to rate premiums. We assume here that the credit is applicable to a standard benefits package that does not vary. (We consider the effect of differing plan generosities somewhat in our second model.) Setting the loading for individual insurance initially at 30 percent of premiums, we then reduce the "net" loading by the amount of the tax credit and assume that the proportion of (otherwise identical) individuals who will buy individual insurance at any given loading is at least as much as the proportion that would have purchased group insurance at the same loading.

To determine this proportion, we first estimate a probit model of the likelihood of being privately insured as a function of the net loading (based on tax rates and industry-level firm size), as well as multiple other control variables posited to be correlated with both the demand for insurance and the average net loading that families face; most importantly, these variables include family income, education, and age.[4] (We do not control for the size of the firm the person actually works for, since people with weak tastes for insurance would be expected to choose to work for small firms, thus biasing the estimates.) Results of this estimation are shown in Table 2. The overall results from this demand estimation essentially indicate for each individual a predicted probability of being insured as a function of his various demographics and the net loading he faces. Thus, the effect of facing a lower net loading can be simulated simply by giving each individual the lesser of his family's current group net loading or the credited nongroup net loading. This then generates for each individual (whose credited premium is lower than his tax-subsidized group premium) a new predicted probability of being insured as a function of the proportional tax credit.

Using this Model One methodology, the estimated effects of tax credits of 25, 33, 50, 66, and 75 percent of the individual insurance premium (assumed to have loading equal to 30 percent of premiums) are shown in the top half of Table 3. Results are shown for all income levels and for both low- and high-income levels separately, where we define low and high income as total family income either below or above 300 percent of the poverty level adjusted for family size. Again, because the net loading under group insurance is generally much less than that under individual insurance, it will take a fairly sizeable credit to prompt the uninsured who rejected a group insurance option to begin to buy insurance.[5] For example, we find that if the credit is 25 percent of individual insurance premiums, virtually the only persons who will be newly enticed into the market will be some of those self-employed whose only option before was nongroup insurance.

Among low-income workers and dependents, the current proportion uninsured is 30.7 percent. Smaller tax credits do not do much good in reducing the number of low-income uninsured, but a 50 percent credit reduces this proportion by 51.8 percent (to 14.8 percent uninsured), and a credit of two-thirds of the premium would cause three-fourths (74.2 percent) of these low-income uninsured to seek coverage. The proportion uninsured among higher-income workers and dependents starts out lower (at 10.3 percent) and falls less dramatically to 5.0 percent at a credit equal to half of their nongroup premium.

Results shown in the bottom panel of Table 3 instead use the assumption that administrative loading in the individual insurance market is 40 percent of premiums. (For reasons discussed in Pauly et al. 1999, loadings in this market may reasonably be assumed to fall in the range of 30 to 40 percent.) Clearly, the higher net price here induces fewer individuals to become insured. And since the loading in the nongroup market has an important impact on the effectiveness of tax credits in stimulating the purchase of insurance, the current uncertainty about what this loading is or could be will significantly affect estimates of the effects of credits.

Of course, as we have noted, some individuals who are currently insured through their employers—particularly those with low incomes in small groups who experience low marginal tax rates and high administrative loading—will also take advantage of these tax credits. The final column of Table 3 shows the number of currently group-insured who would use credits for the individual market. With lower credits, few individuals drop group coverage, because their tax-advantaged group price is lower than those generated by the individual insurance tax credits. But larger credits can cause a substantial number of individuals to switch to individual insurance and increase the credits' "cost per newly insured," though as we have noted, such costs are properly viewed as transfers of wealth. (In our simulation model, a large number of high-income individuals take advantage of these credits simply because we have included no income-related eligibility criteria for the use of these credits in our model. Such criteria are likely to be advocated by policymakers on grounds of equity and should be easily implemented without resulting distortions in behavior.) Most importantly, there is only a narrow window of tax credit values in which additional coverage is stimulated but group insurance is not decimated. Of course, if equal credits were offered regardless of how and whether insurance is initially obtained, there would be a much smaller switch out of group coverage but more "cost" (again, actually transfers) the government would pay to taxpayers.

Model Two

Our first model obviously assumes that behavior in the group market translates to the individual market; it does not pay attention to individual characteristics that may make seeking insurance compared to being uninsured more or less attractive. A second model, to compare with the results of the first, attempts to estimate reservation prices directly, by examining variations in individual risk levels (based on expected out-of-pocket expenses). We assume that a currently uninsured person whose available premium is reduced by a tax credit will choose to be insured if the utility of buying insurance is higher for him than it would be if he remained uninsured. The credit is usually less than the assumed individual insurance premium; so the person will only buy if the gain from becoming insured (reservation price) is less than the net premium to be paid. In general, the gain from becoming insured has four components: a reduction in expected out-of-pocket payments with insurance, a reduction in costs associated with either receiving charity care or with bill collection and bankruptcy for unpaid bills, a reduction in risk due to the variation in out-of-pocket expenses, and the value of the additional care used because of "moral hazard" (that is, the incentive to receive low-value care that third-party payment creates).

To model the choice of purchasing insurance versus remaining uninsured, we use a simulation model based upon this expected utility theory that is quite similar to one we developed for determining individual choice between two insurance plans differing in generosity (Pauly and Herring 2000). We start with the distribution of actual expenses (both total and out-of-pocket) for currently uninsured individuals aged eighteen to sixty-four in the MEPS data (N = 2,218). Next we generate a distribution of expenses (total and out-of-pocket) for these individuals as if they were insured in a benchmark policy. We begin with considering a fairly comprehensive benchmark policy—one with a $200 deductible, 20 percent coinsurance, and a $1,500 out-of-pocket maximum. To inflate the uninsured expenses to insured expenses for this set of currently insured adults, we use the American Academy of Actuaries (1995) "induction" methodology, which employs a set of "moral hazard" induction parameters to adjust total expenses based upon the change in out-of-pocket costs.

We also generate an alternative pair of uninsured and insured expense distributions by starting with the expenses for currently insured persons in the MEPS data (N = 7,598) and reducing their expenses with this AAA methodology to what they would be if they were uninsured. In determining what proportion of total uninsured expenses would be paid out of pocket, we use results from Herring (2000) which document (by income level) how the proportion of expenses paid out of pocket decreases as the magnitude of total expenses increases. For the results using this deflated expense distribution from the currently insured, the sample is reweighted to be consistent with differences in age, gender, and health status between the insured and uninsured.

Then for each uninsured individual (either each currently uninsured individual in the MEPS or each reweighted currently insured individual in the MEPS with deflated total expenses) we determine his reservation price directly as the sum of the following three or four components: the change in expected out-of-pocket expenses if he were insured, the change in risk due to the variation in out-of-pocket expenses, the change in consumer surplus, and (in some estimates) a change in utility associated with avoiding charity care and/or bad debt. As in our prior simulation of insurance choice (Pauly and Herring 2000), the individual's expected expenses are determined by a weighted average of his actual expense and his average "cell" expense, where we define twenty cells based upon the interaction of five ten-year age intervals, gender, and excellent or very good self-reported health status versus good, fair, or poor. We assume the utility gain associated with avoiding charity and bad debt equals a proportion (averaging around 30 percent, but increasing with income level) of the total amount received free; this is similar in spirit to the modeling of the disutility associated with managed care restrictions in Keeler et al. (1996). We estimate the valuation of risk as one-half the Arrow-Pratt absolute risk aversion coefficient times the variance in out-of-pocket costs. We use a coefficient of 0.00095 (equal to that used in our prior simulations of insurance choice) and apply this to the "cost" of receiving free care when applicable. Finally, we estimate the value of consuming additional care as one-half times the change in expected total expense.

The resulting reservation prices we estimate then vary considerably, depending on which of the two methods we use to generate predicted expenses and on which assumption we make about the utility "cost" of bad debt and/or charity care. If we use the uninsured's original expense distribution inflated to give an insured distribution and assume no disutility from receiving free care, we generate a reservation price for the uninsured that averages $128; if we assume a cost of receiving free care averaging thirty cents per dollar, we generate an average reservation price of $566. Using instead the reweighted currently insured's expense distribution deflated to give an uninsured expense distribution generates larger reservation prices: an average of $230 with "cost-less" free care and an average of $1,348 with costly free care.[6] But in each of these four cases, the way that the estimated reservation prices vary with respect to age, gender, and health status is identical. As one would expect, the willingness to pay for insurance increases with characteristics predicting higher medical expense: female gender, older age, and health status reported as good, fair, or poor.

Finally, we assume that the individual insurance premium is risk rated based on age and gender only, and then generate our estimates by determining average benefits for this benchmark policy using the AAA-adjusted distribution of expenses of the MEPS currently insured and marking them up assuming 30 percent administrative loading. The top half of Table 4 presents results of the reduction in the number of uninsured for proportional tax credits of 25, 33, 50, 66, and 75 percent of the individual insurance premium for each of the four cases described above.

For either assumption on the source of the predicted expense distribution, the effects of proportional credits on insurance purchases for people who attach no disutility to charity care and/or bad debt are quite small—a credit of 50 percent leads to only 1.3 to 2.7 percent of the uninsured switching. Those who do switch are predominantly those with poor health. The reason for this small effect is that the data indicate that insurance coverage has a very modest impact on out-of-pocket payments for the uninsured. Those who are uninsured currently pay out of pocket on average for about 30 percent of the cost of their care. Under the benchmark policy that fraction is only reduced to 15 to 20 percent, while the premium charged must cover the cost of all insured care, including that which was formerly "free."

By contrast, if people do prefer to avoid incurring bills they cannot pay, the credits have impacts in the range of the estimates generated by Model One. Even using the uninsured's inflated expense distribution, the proportion of uninsured who become covered is 30.3 percent under a 50 percent proportional credit and 68.4 percent with a 75 percent credit. Those across both genders and all age groups take up insurance using these proportional credits, but within each age/gender "cell," those with poor health are more likely to switch. For credits of 50 percent and larger, there is nearly complete switching if we instead use the insured's inflated expense distribution. These results show the range of possible effects that proportional credits may have, and show the importance of the attitudes of nonpoor uninsured people about free care.

We also estimate the effects of fixed-dollar credits equal in average cost to the proportional credits described above. As shown in the bottom half of Table 4, such credits generally have much more of an effect. Under the most conservative assumptions, 30.9 percent become newly insured with a $689 fixed-dollar credit (in 1996 dollars) that would cover half of an average individual insurance premium for those who are currently uninsured. Since a fixed credit covers a larger proportion of the age-adjusted premium, the newly insured are largely young persons of both genders, including many of those with less than good health. Attaching disutility to free care increases the estimated impact, but not by as much as in the proportional case. Generally, larger fixed-dollar credits of about $1,000 (in 1996 dollars) are estimated to be used by at the least half of the uninsured.

4

An Optimal Partial Coverage Policy

Thus far we have limited our analysis to only fairly comprehensive plans and tax credits that would cover some portion of their premiums. Now we will consider the possibility that a fixed credit can be used by individuals to purchase any policy they want. In other words, what kind of limited-coverage policy would the uninsured obtain if they just used the credit and none of their own money to buy insurance? To estimate such an optimal insurance policy, we proceed by first determining combinations of deductibles and upper limits on total benefits that a given tax subsidy could cover for a particular uninsured individual. Then, given the set of financially feasible policies, we determine the expected utility for each deductible and upper limit pair and select the one with the highest expected utility.

We concentrate on females between the ages of eighteen and thirty-nine. Relative to the variation in expected medical expenses across all adults under age sixty-five, the variation in expected expenses within this group is small, and the average expense of this sub-population is close to the average across all nonelderly adults. First, we take the distribution of expenses of all currently insured females aged eighteen to thirty-nine in the 1996 MEPS data (N = 1,835), and for various deductibles find the corresponding upper limit on benefits such that total benefits equal exactly $700, which gives an individual insurance premium of $1,000 (in 1996 dollars), assuming there is 30 percent administrative loading. In doing so, we again use the AAA methodology described above to generate a realistic expense distribution for each particular deductible and upper limit pair. Compared to average total expenses of about $1,577 for "fully insured" younger females in the 1996 MEPS data, we estimate their total expenses would fall to about $1,220 in these "partially insured" policies—leaving about $520 on average to be paid out of pocket (some of which is above the deductible and some of which is above the upper limit). There is some variation in these $1,220 and $520 amounts because the different deductible and upper limit pairs have slightly different effects on total expenses when the moral hazard adjustment is made. Various financially feasible combinations of deductibles and upper limits are shown in the first two columns of Table 5. For instance, $1,000 could purchase first-dollar coverage with a $1,616.90 upper limit, a $1,000 deductible paired with a $7,375.20 upper limit, or a $1,974.20 deductible with no upper limit.

For each feasible policy, we then determine its expected utility incorporating the same framework as Model Two—that is, examining the plan's expected out-of-pocket expenses, valuation of risk, and consumer surplus. What makes examining these upper limits on benefits interesting is the potential for these "partially insured" individuals to obtain free care once they surpass their policy's upper limit, thus lowering both the magnitude of and variation in out-of-pocket expense. We consider two cases. The first assumes that individuals will receive no free care at all. For the second case, we use Herring's (2000) results for the proportions that the uninsured pay out of pocket as total expense increases and income varies. Generalizing for those with incomes between 200 and 250 percent of the poverty line and adjusting downward the amount received free for moderately sized bills, we assume that those who exceed their upper limit but have total expenses under $20,000 can expect to pay out of pocket for only half of the remaining costs and assume that those whose bills exceed the upper limit and are larger than $20,000 pay out of pocket for 4.5 percent of the remainder.

Based upon these varying assumptions, we can then calculate the expected utility of each policy as one and a half times the total expected expense, minus the sum of the expected out-of-pocket expense, the "cost" of free care, and the valuation of risk. Consider first the case where individuals can expect to receive no free care once their upper limit is exceeded. Expected out-of-pocket expenses, valuations of risk, and resulting expected utilities are shown in the upper half of Table 5 for various feasible policies. As one would expect, the risk of paying large out-of-pocket expenses once a person exceeds the upper limit on total benefits increases exponentially as that upper limit decreases. Thus, for this case of no free care availability, utility is maximized when there is no upper limit on benefits: Utility of $1,080.90 is expected when a deductible of $1,974.20 is chosen with full coverage above that deductible.

Results for the second case, where we make the assumptions described above about the availability of free care after one exceeds the upper limit, are shown in the bottom portion of Table 5. Here, utility is maximized at $1,200.60 for a deductible of $525 and an upper limit of $4,072. This optimal policy is one that trades off the cost from raising the deductible and hence paying more out of pocket to cover the deductible versus the benefit from raising the upper limit to a value closer to an amount at which free care and/or bad debt increasingly covers larger bills.

This analysis should make clear that by permitting a reduction in the generosity of the required coverage needed to qualify for the tax credit, all individuals would be expected to (rationally) purchase at least some limited form of insurance coverage, and thus take-up rates of the uninsured should be 100 percent. But here, too, what particular plan is optimal for a particular individual depends critically upon his expected medical expenses, risk aversion, and both the ability and attitudes of individuals in regard to obtaining free care.

5

Conclusions

Many different proposals have been made for adding refundable tax credits and reforming the tax treatment of employer-paid group health insurance. The options considered in this paper, like most current proposals, do not require individuals or firms to pay higher taxes if they continue to provide employer-paid insurance. (See Pauly and Goodman 1995 for an early discussion of this issue.) The possibility that some employers or firms may be required to pay higher taxes yields the result, in some analyses, that tax credit proposals might cause some people currently receiving group coverage to drop it (Cox and Topoleski 1999); these analyses are largely irrelevant to the present debate on tax credit options. Those schemes that do envision removing or limiting the current tax subsidy also assume there will be a mandate (individual, employer, or employer-enforced individual) to obtain subsidized coverage (Butler 1991, Pauly et al. 1992).

The Key Tradeoff

Our simulation estimates serve to illustrate numerically a key tradeoff suggested earlier. For a given amount "spent" on credits, there is a tradeoff between the *breadth* of the reduction in the number of uninsured and the *depth* of the increase in the coverage they take. There is also an interaction with risk levels. At one extreme, a flat credit that does not specify a minimum policy will cause all of the previously uninsured to obtain some insurance coverage. At very low risk levels, the previously uninsured will probably be able to buy coverage society would regard as "adequate." (There is no objective standard for "adequate coverage.") But persons with high risks who are unwilling or unable to pay

25

more of the premium themselves will have to select coverage with deductibles and (especially) upper limits. While the new coverage will provide both more protection against out-of-pocket payments and more encouragement for the use of beneficial care, the protection and encouragement will obviously be smaller than if nominal coverage were more generous.

Under a policy of fixed-dollar credits and a requirement to buy an "adequate" benchmark policy, some of the uninsured will reject the subsidy and remain uninsured. Persons with lower risks and those who place high value on avoiding being a charity or bad debt case will move to coverage which, by definition, is "adequate." Compared to the alternative policy discussed in the previous paragraph, this policy will convert fewer people from uninsured to insured, but among those who are converted we will see a larger effect on their use of and protection by health insurance.

Finally, a policy of proportional credits will move fewer people out of the ranks of the uninsured, but, of those it does cause to become insured, more will come from the higher risk categories. But such a policy may also stimulate (and subsidize) the purchase of coverage in excess of the benchmark level; it could lead to "lavish plans," especially among those who were formerly insured but can become eligible for the credit.

Which of these three alternatives is best? The answer clearly cannot be given with objective certainty; it all depends on how the different patterns of changes are valued. If one invokes the principle that the first few dollars of insurance coverage (like the first few dollars of anything beneficial) are likely to do the most good, a design that places rather light obligations on the comprehensiveness of coverage and uses fixed-dollar credits may make sense. But ultimately the choice itself will require consensus on exactly why "we" want the uninsured to become insured, and what benefits we expect to accrue to all from that change.

Another key issue when choosing tax credit options is how generous the credit is to be. At a given income level, small credits will have little effect on the number of uninsured, whereas large credits will have large effects. If we focus on the large majority of the uninsured who have incomes above the poverty line, our general conclusion is that credits will need to be substantial to make much of a dent in the number of uninsured. For low-income workers (and their dependents) below 300 percent of the poverty line (where the uninsured are disproportionately found), we conclude that substantial reductions in the numbers of uninsured will require credits in the range of approximately half of the individual insurance premiums, with even greater credits needed for families with incomes at the bottom of this range. Thus another important tradeoff occurs between reductions in the number of the uninsured versus tax revenues that could be spent on other public programs.

But note that much of the "cost" of tax credits does not represent a reallocation of real resources away from other uses and toward the health care needs of the previously uninsured. Instead, much of the credit effectively represents a tax reduction for the majority of lower-middle-income people who formerly had obtained health insurance for themselves and their families in some fashion. Limiting eligibility for the credit to a subset of those at the same income level engaging in the same health insurance purchasing behavior can reduce the "cost," but at the real expense of horizontal inequity and substantial distortion in the labor market.

To make any such judgments rationally, however, one would need more information than just a head count of the formerly uninsured. The missing piece of information is important for the entire policy exercise: How much of an improvement in health is generated by the presence of insurance coverage (compared to its absence) for people at different income and risk levels? It is possible, for example, that insurance coverage for people who are initially low risks may produce more of an improvement in health than coverage for those who are initially high risks. Almost all of the research on the impact of insurance coverage either looks at the uninsured as a group or singles out poor uninsured people, but the most relevant question is the amount of good that health insurance would produce for a lower-middle-income family (compared to their being uninsured). As noted elsewhere by Pauly and Reinhardt (1996), our failure as researchers to produce this information on effectiveness makes it more difficult to persuade our fellow citizens to support tax credits or any other programs to reduce the numbers of the uninsured.

The fiscal design of tax credit programs is not the only influence on the number of uninsured. Most programs envision making everyone who is uninsured (at some income level) eligible for subsidy. This design stands in strong contrast to the Medicaid program, for which only some low-income uninsured are eligible. The universal character of tax credit programs would thus allow the government to direct subsidies or credit vouchers to everyone below a certain income level who is not insured; it would not be necessary for people to apply. In addition, once people at some income level had all been made eligible for credits judged to provide adequate subsidies to permit them to afford insurance, there would be less justification for someone to remain uninsured, and therefore less need to have a permissive charity care or bad debt policy applied to that person. Changes in the financial responsibilities imposed on uninsured people might themselves stimulate people to become insured, although some safety net will need to remain for those who truly fall through the cracks. Finally, rewarding the great majority of lower-middle-income people who do choose to be insured with a substantial tax reduction might both call attention to the social value of being insured and offer the uninsured further incentive to change their status. While it is unlikely that the number of uninsured will ever be literally zero, carefully designed credit programs can both reduce the numbers of uninsured and improve the equity of tax treatment of the insured.

Statistical Appendix

TABLE 1

Insurance Status for the U.S. Population: Full-time Workers and Their Dependents

| | All Individuals | Percent of Population | | |
		Excluding Public	Privately Insured	The Uninsured
All Income				
Public insurance[a]	9.6	0.0	0.0	0.0
Current job offers insurance[b]	77.6	80.9	91.7	38.1
Private insurance	72.1	79.8	100.0	0.0
Employment-based	67.8	74.9	94.0	0.0
Nongroup insurance	4.4	4.8	6.0	0.0
Uninsured	18.3	20.2	0.0	100.0
200%–250% of Poverty Line				
Public insurance	8.8	0.0	0.0	0.0
Current job offers insurance	80.0	80.5	91.2	41.6
Private insurance	71.6	78.5	100.0	0.0
Employment-based	67.7	74.3	94.6	0.0
Nongroup insurance	3.8	4.2	5.4	0.0
Uninsured	19.6	21.5	0.0	100.0

Note: Since many individuals have more than one source of insurance, "hierarchical" assumptions were made in that public coverage dominates private coverage and group coverage dominates nongroup coverage.

a. Public insurance includes Medicaid, Medicare, CHAMPUS, or any other federal or state program subsidizing coverage.

b. Some individuals have employment-based coverage but are not offered insurance through their *current* job, e.g., COBRA-continuation coverage or group coverage through a family member working *part-time*.

Source: 1996 Medical Expenditure Panel Survey Data (N = 13,344).

TABLE 2

Model One: Probability of Being Insured as a Function of Net Loading and Other Controls

Variable	Mean	Probit Coefficient
Insured / Intercept	0.798	-2.529 ***
Net loading	-0.024	-1.767 ***
Family income's percentage of poverty[a]	377.5	0.337 ***
Highest family education level	13.33	0.099 ***
Nonwhite	0.269	-0.365 ***
Male ages 0–9	0.070	0.456 ***
Male ages 10–17	0.065	0.358 ***
Male ages 18–24	0.047	-0.214 ***
Male ages 25–34	0.103	n/a
Male ages 35–44	0.108	0.295 ***
Male ages 45–54	0.079	0.446 ***
Male ages 55–64	0.038	0.585 ***
Female ages 0–9	0.069	0.462 ***
Female ages 10–17	0.062	0.474 ***
Female ages 18–24	0.045	-0.064
Female ages 25–34	0.095	0.284 ***
Female ages 35–44	0.106	0.485 ***

Female ages 45–54	0.078	0.623 ***
Female ages 55–64	0.034	0.622 ***
Northeast census region	0.188	n/a
Midwest census region	0.229	0.100 **
South census region	0.361	-0.089 **
West census region	0.221	0.046
Urban area	0.813	0.051
Number of observations	11,564	11,564
Log likelihood	n/a	-4584.4

Note: Sample includes all full-time workers and their dependents up to age sixty-four, excluding those with any form of public insurance.

a. A logged value of the total family income as a percentage of the poverty level, adjusted for family size, is used in the probit model estimation.

*** Significant at 0.01 or better
** Significant at between 0.01 and 0.05
* Significant at between 0.05 and 0.10

Source: 1996 Medical Expenditure Panel Survey Data.

TABLE 3

Model One: Effect of Tax Credits on the Uninsured, All Full-time Workers and Dependents

	Predicted Percent Insured	Percent Newly Insured	Percent Reduction in Uninsured	Group Insured Dropping
Assuming nongroup loading equals 30% of premiums				
All income levels				
Currently	80.0	n/a	n/a	n/a
25% credit	82.6	2.6	13.0	2.8
33% credit	84.0	4.1	20.2	34.7
50% credit	90.3	10.4	51.7	100.0
66% credit	95.1	15.1	75.5	100.0
75% credit	96.6	16.7	83.2	100.0
Low income—below 300% of poverty line				
Currently	69.3	n/a	n/a	n/a
25% credit	72.7	3.4	11.1	6.8
33% credit	75.5	6.2	20.0	79.0
50% credit	85.2	15.9	51.8	100.0
66% credit	92.1	22.8	74.2	100.0
75% credit	94.4	25.1	81.9	100.0
High income—above 300% of poverty line				
Currently	89.7	n/a	n/a	n/a
25% credit	91.5	1.9	18.0	0.0

33% credit	91.8	2.1	20.8	3.5
50% credit	95.0	5.3	51.5	100.0
66% credit	97.8	8.2	79.1	100.0
75% credit	98.6	9.0	86.9	100.0
Assuming nongroup loading equals 40% of premiums				
All income levels				
25% credit	81.8	1.8	9.1	0.0
33% credit	82.4	2.4	12.0	1.0
50% credit	86.9	6.9	34.7	76.6
66% credit	93.8	13.8	69.0	100.0
75% credit	95.9	16.0	79.7	100.0
Low income—below 300% of poverty line				
25% credit	71.6	2.2	7.3	0.0
33% credit	72.4	3.1	10.1	2.5
50% credit	80.5	11.2	36.5	100.0
66% credit	90.1	20.8	67.9	100.0
75% credit	93.4	24.0	78.3	100.0
High income—above 300% of poverty line				
25% credit	91.1	1.4	13.9	0.0
33% credit	91.4	1.8	17.2	50.0
50% credit	92.7	3.1	29.6	60.2
66% credit	97.1	7.4	71.9	100.0
75% credit	98.3	8.6	83.4	100.0

Note: Details of the simulation are provided in chap. 3.

TABLE 4

Model Two: Effect of Tax Credits on the Currently Uninsured, Comprehensive Individual Insurance Plan with 30 Percent Loading[a]

| | Reduction in the Uninsured (in %) | | | |
| | Originally Uninsured Inflated Expense Distribution | | Originally Insured Deflated Expense Distribution | |
	Costless Free Care	Costly Free Care	Costless Free Care	Costly Free Care
Proportional credits				
25% credit	0.7	12.0	0.8	65.9
33% credit	1.0	17.0	1.1	72.5
50% credit	1.3	30.3	2.7	84.7
66% credit	3.6	51.9	13.9	94.3
75% credit	8.7	68.4	27.7	96.9
Fixed-dollar credits (1996 dollars)				
$345 (~ 25%)	2.2	27.6	7.7	66.3
$459 (~ 33%)	15.0	36.2	21.0	70.6
$689 (~ 50%)	30.9	53.0	42.0	78.0
$918 (~ 66%)	49.2	59.0	54.4	84.9
$1,034 (~ 75%)	53.6	60.9	54.8	87.8

Note: Details of the simulation are provided in chap. 3.

a. Comprehensive plan assumes a $200 deductible, 20% coinsurance, and a $1,500 maximum out-of-pocket expenses.

TABLE 5

An Optimal Partial Coverage Policy:
Premium Equaling $1,000 for Females Aged 18 to 39[a]

Assuming No Free Care Is Available after Exceeding Upper Limit

Deductible	Upper Limit	Amount of Free Care	Out-of-pocket Expense	Valuation of Risk	Expected Utility
$0.0	$1,616.9	$0.0	$506.4	$4,961.8	$-3,658.6
100.0	2095.1	0.0	525.0	4,843.0	-3,530.5
250.0	2,790.5	0.0	539.0	4,691.4	-3,371.9
500.0	3,951.3	0.0	546.5	4,480.0	-3,156.7
1,000.0	7,375.2	0.0	536.5	4,013.6	-2,695.4
1,500.0	22,625.0	0.0	521.3	2,861.4	-1,550.8
1,750.0	62,747.7	0.0	507.5	1,141.9	161.9
1,950.0	12,1370.6	0.0	496.1	280.6	1,017.5
1,974.2	None	0.0	494.8	216.5	1,080.9

Assuming Some Free Care Is Available after Exceeding Upper Limit

Deductible	Upper Limit	Amount of Free Care	Out-of-Pocket Expense	Valuation of Risk	Expected Utility
$0.0	$1616.9	$298.4	$208.0	$357.8	$1154.3
100.0	2,095.1	268.2	256.8	331.7	1,168.4
250.0	2,790.5	232.1	306.9	304.5	1,177.5
500.0	3,951.3	189.0	357.5	277.6	1,177.9
525.0	4,072.0	191.3	355.1	256.6	1,200.6
550.0	4,197.0	187.6	358.6	254.6	1,199.8
1,000.0	7,375.2	133.4	403.1	221.9	1,189.8
1,500.0	22,625.0	74.8	446.4	201.8	1,161.2
1,974.2	None	0.0	494.8	216.5	1,080.9

Note: All amounts are in 1996 dollars. Details of the analysis—particularly the calculation of expected utility—are provided in chap. 4.

a. Policy is assumed to have no coinsurance and administrative loading equals 30 percent of premiums.

Notes

1. The MEPS data—at least what is publicly available—does not indicate whether workers offered coverage were offered single or family coverage; so this represents somewhat of an upper bound for workers *and* dependents offered coverage. Yet according to the 1993 Robert Wood Johnson Employer Survey, over 97 percent of firms offering insurance offer family coverage, and so we consider these 41.6 and 38.1 percent estimates to be reliable. Thus, many uninsured dependents of workers offered coverage are indeed forgoing insurance as well—although perhaps at a substantial fraction of the total premium.

2. These are each average amounts obtained from the MEPS Insurance Component data.

3. This calculation is even likely to be an understatement of the size of the tax subsidy because it is believed that the incidence of the employer's payroll tax of 8 percent is on wages as well. But for our purposes here, and further below, we only consider the employee-paid payroll tax.

4. We estimate one model using the full sample of workers and their dependents not covered by public insurance, and thus we are not able to obtain different coefficients for the net loading for low- and high-income individuals separately. There is, however, no consensus on how the price elasticity for insurance varies by income: Higher price elasticities for low-income individuals have been documented by both Holmer (1984) and Sheils et al. (1999). On the other hand, Jon Gruber (1999, 39) builds into his simulation model a price elasticity that decreases as income decreases, arguing "that as income falls, individuals are less likely to take up subsidies which are less than 100 percent, as disposable income is needed for other expenditures that may be perceived as more urgent (such as food and housing)." Probit models that we estimated for low- and high-income sub-samples bore no consistent patterns with

respect to this net loading variable; thus, we use the full sample results for increased precision.

5. Indeed, this net loading under the current tax treatment of insurance averages -0.024 across all workers and their dependents; it averages 0.048 for those with low incomes and -0.089 for those with high incomes. This is significantly lower than the net loading of 0.429 in the nongroup market, assuming loading equal to 30 percent of premiums.

6. This discrepancy between the use of the two original expense distributions is related to whether the currently insured—given their age, gender, and health status—would continue to be low consumers of medical care (that is, the AAA methodology allows for the retention of idiosyncratic differences in consumption upon inflating their expenses) or would consume amounts of medical care equal to their insured counterparts—given their age, gender, and health status.

References

American Academy of Actuaries. 1995. "Medical Savings Accounts: Cost Implications and Design Issues." AAA Public Policy Monograph.

Butler, S. 1991. "A Tax Reform Strategy to Deal with the Uninsured." *Journal of the American Medical Association* 265 (19): 2541–44.

Cooper, P., and B. Schone. 1997. "More Offers, Fewer Takers for Employment-based Health Insurance: 1987 and 1996." *Health Affairs* 16 (6): 142–9.

Cox, D., and C. Topoleski. 1999. "Individual Choice Initiatives: Analysis of a Hypothetical Model Act." EBRI-ERF Policy Forum, May 5.

Gruber, J. 1999. "Tax Subsides for Health Insurance: Evaluating the Costs and Benefits." Prepared for the Kaiser Family Foundation.

Herring, B. 2000. "Access to Free Care for the Uninsured and Its Effect on Private Health Insurance Coverage." Doctoral dissertation, University of Pennsylvania.

Holmer, M. 1984. "Tax Policy and the Demand for Health Insurance." *Journal of Health Economics* 3: 203–21.

Keeler, E., J. Malkin, D. Goldman, and J. Buchanan. 1996. "Can Medical Savings Accounts for the Nonelderly Reduce Health Care Costs?" *Journal of the American Medical Association* 275 (21): 1666–71.

Pauly, M., P. Danzon, P. Feldstein, and J. Hoff. 1992. *Responsible National Health Insurance*. Washington, D.C.: AEI Press.

Pauly, M., and J. Goodman. 1995. "Tax Credits for Health Insurance and Medical Savings Accounts." *Health Affairs* 14 (1): 125–39.

Pauly, M., and U. Reinhardt. 1996. "The Rise and Fall of Health Care Reform: A Dialogue between Mark Pauly and Uwe Reinhardt" in *Looking Back, Looking Forward: The Institute of Medicine's Rosenthal Lectures*. Washington, D.C.: National Academy Press.

Pauly, M., and B. Herring. 1999. *Pooling Health Insurance Risks*. Washington, D.C.: AEI Press.

Pauly, M., and B. Herring. 2000. "An Efficient Employer Strategy for Dealing with Adverse Selection in Multiple-plan Offerings: An MSA Example." *Journal of Health Economics* 19 (4): 513–28.

Pauly, M., A. Percy, and B. Herring. 1999. "Individual Versus Job-based Health Insurance: Weighing the Pros and Cons." *Health Affairs* 18 (6): 28–44.

Phelps, C.. 1997. *Health Economics*. Reading, Mass.: Addison, Wesley.

Sheils, J., P. Hogan, and R. Haught. 1999. "Health Insurance and Taxes: The Impact of Proposed Changes in Current Federal Policy." Prepared for the National Coalition on Health Care.

About the Authors

MARK V. PAULY is a professor of health care systems, insurance and risk management, and public policy and management at the Wharton School, a professor of economics at the School of Arts and Sciences, and Bendheim Professor, all at the University of Pennsylvania. He is a member of the Institute of Medicine and an adjunct scholar of AEI.

Mr. Pauly was the director of research and the executive director of the Leonard Davis Institute of Health Economics; a visiting research fellow at the International Institute of Management; a commissioner of the Physical Payment Review Commission; and a professor of economics at Northwestern University. He is on numerous editorial boards and has written more than one hundred journal articles.

He is the author of *Responsible Tax Credits for Health Insurance* (AEI Press, 2002, with John S. Hoff), *Pooling Health Insurance Risks* (AEI Press, 1999, with Mr. Herring), *Financing Long-Term Care: What Should Be the Government's Role?* (AEI Press, 1996, with Peter Zweifel), and *An Analysis of Medical Savings Accounts: Do Two Wrongs Make a Right?* (AEI Press, 1994).

BRADLEY HERRING is a Robert Wood Johnson Foundation Health Policy Scholar at Yale University's Institution for Social and Policy Studies. Mr. Herring's research focuses on economic and public policy issues related to private health insurance and the uninsured. His publications include the book *Pooling Health Insurance Risks* (AEI Press, 1999, with Mr. Pauly) and articles in *Health Affairs* and the *Journal of Health Economics*.